The Portuguese Explorers

In 1434 Captain Gil Eanes sailed safely beyond Cape Bojador and the age of Portuguese exploration and empire began.

Walter Buehr takes us back through history on the voyages of the great explorers such as Bartolomeo Diaz and Vasco da Gama. We witness the excitement of discovery of new lands, of great riches in the golden cities of India and the East Indies, the Spice Islands and China.

To Prince Henry the Navigator belongs the greatest glory. It was his captains who explored the western coast of Africa almost to the equator, who discovered all the islands off Portugal and the currents of the open Atlantic. It was Prince Henry who developed the science of navigation.

Here is the story of the brave men who gave Portugal domination of the seas for over a century.

The Portuguese Explorers

by WALTER BUEHR

G. P. Putnam's Sons   New York

Published simultaneously in the Dominion of
Canada by Longmans Canada, Limited, Toronto

Library of Congress Catalog Card Number: 66-10452
PRINTED IN THE UNITED STATES OF AMERICA
08212

Contents

The Portuguese Explorers

Centuries ago the sea-faring sons of Portugal sailed their frail little galleys, barcas, carracks and caravels to the undiscovered islands and wild coasts of half the world. They ranged from the cold, foggy harbors of Newfoundland and the tropical shores of Brazil, in America, and on the other side of the Atlantic around the tip of Africa to the golden cities of India and the

East Indies, to the Spice Islands, to Cathay, which we call China, and even to the islands of Cipangu, the Japanese Empire.

How did it happen that these Portuguese navigators, setting out from Lisbon, Oporto and Lagos, in little impoverished Portugal, were willing to brave the perils of the unknown below the southern horizon in order to blaze new trails long before the mariners of France, England, Spain and Holland would venture very far from their home ports? The answer lay in the dreams and imagination of one man, Prince Henry, third son of King John of Portugal, who was tortured all his life by the desire to know what lay beyond that far horizon. From 1420 to 1434 he organized expeditions paid out of his own pocket, to sail ever southward along the African coast to find out what lay beyond. Time after time Henry was disappointed when his vessels returned without having passed south of Cape Bojador on the African coast, because the superstitious crews feared what lay beyond.

At the beginning of the fifteenth century it was believed by most seafarers that if they sailed south or west of Bojador they would enter upon a region of wild storms, boiling seas, huge reptiles which could destroy a ship with one crush of their terrible jaws, and remorseless currents which would prevent a ship from ever returning. It was rumored that there were magnetic rocks that set compass needles to whirling and kept the navigators from laying out a course. Many people still believed that the earth was shaped like a

great flat plate, and that any ship approaching the rim
would be swept to destruction over the waterfalls roar-
ing over the edge. The sun was believed to be so hot
in the south, as witness the evidence that the people
from below the Sahara were so dark, that any white

man venturing there would be burned to a crisp. It was easy to understand why the mariners were so reluctant to range farther south.

Prince Henry had another reason, stronger than curiosity, for sending out his expeditions. The mapmakers and geographers of his time believed that Africa was much smaller than it turned out to be. They believed that if a ship survived the terrors lurking in the sea she could quickly sail around the southern coast of Africa into the Indian Ocean and reach the fabulous East Indies, with their gold, rubies and pearls, and above all, the rich products of the Spice Islands.

You have seen the condiment shelves in the supermarkets, with their long rows of small jars and cans labeled Ginger, Nutmeg or Pepper, marked with low prices and perhaps have wondered why spices were so eagerly sought and so expensive and hard to get in the fifteenth century. Spices were so much more important then because the cooks of the 1400's had no refrigeration; when they butchered an animal the meat had to be cooked and eaten at once, or salted, pickled or dried, lest it spoil. Also choices were much more limited; many of our common vegetables like potatoes, carrots and spinach were unknown in Europe in the fifteenth century. There were no glass jars in which to preserve those they had, and of course canned foods would not appear for four hundred years.

In winter a diet of salted or pickled meat, cabbage, turnips and bread could become very monotonous, so the cooks mixed many kinds of spices in most of their dishes, if they could afford them, to make them more tasteful. Most fifteenth century dishes would be far too spicy for our taste today. Heavy spicing was also used to conceal the "high" flavor of most meat dishes, since meat began to turn bad very soon after butchering. Spices were also in demand by doctors and apothecaries, who used them in concocting their medicines. They were also needed by perfumers.

Salt and some spices could be found in Europe, but many existed only in the Moluccas, or Spice Islands, between Borneo and New Guinea, whose locations were known only to the Arab traders. Some of the spices used in fifteenth century kitchens were cinnamon, pepper, ginger, mint, cardamom, galingale, nutmeg, sage, parsley, caraway seed, saffron, anise, almonds, cloves, myrrh and mace.

Spices were very costly in Europe because they came by ship and camel caravan, over routes entirely controlled by the Arabs and Turks, who could charge what they pleased or cut off the supply at any time. Every trader, caravaneer, and Arabian dhow-captain who handled the merchandise demanded his profit, and it was taxed heavily at each frontier. This of course added to the cost; in the 14th century, for example, two hundred pounds of pepper cost 50 English pounds laid down at the docks of Marseilles, France, and 70 to 80 pounds by the time it reached England. At today's values, the pepper cost several thousand dollars.

If you look at the map illustrating the Arab trade routes you can see what a long, costly journey a shipment of spices had to make from the Spice Islands to Europe. First, spices were transported from the islands by Malayan, Chinese or Arabian dhows or sailing ships, to Calicut or some other Indian port, where they were transferred into larger vessels for the long voyage across the Indian Ocean, either to Malinda or Mombasa in Africa, or to Aden in Arabia. From Aden they might go by boat to the head of the Red Sea, transfer to camels as far as Cairo in Egypt, and again by ship to Genoa, Venice or Marseilles. Other shipments might be ferried across the Red Sea and then travel by caravan across the trackless sands of the vast sunparched Sahara desert to Timbuktoo, from which smaller caravans branched off to Safi, Tangier, Ceuta, Algiers, Tunis and Tripoli. European traders called at these Moorish ports to buy the spices and carried them by ship to France and England.

A sea route around the coast of Africa, as it then was thought to be, and across the Indian Ocean, would not only have been quicker, but would have saved the con-

stant loading and unloading from ship to caravan and would have avoided the heavy tolls and taxes imposed at every border.

Arab seamen had been sailing down the east coast of Africa from Aden and from India, but they had never ventured farther south, beyond Mozambique, or as far as the Cape of Good Hope, along the east coast. The whole west coast of Africa from the Straits of Gibraltar to the Cape was a land of mystery and unimagined terrors to the European seaman of the early fifteenth century. Actually, two thousand years before, Phoenician sailors, sent by the King of Egypt, had made a three year voyage down the Red Sea, all the way around Africa, and back to Egypt by way of the Mediterranean. Nobody ever repeated the trip, and by the 1400's it had been forgotten.

At the beginning of the fifteenth century none of the maritime nations had ventured south of the Straits of Gibraltar, partly because of the wild tales of the dangers at sea, and partly because they thought there

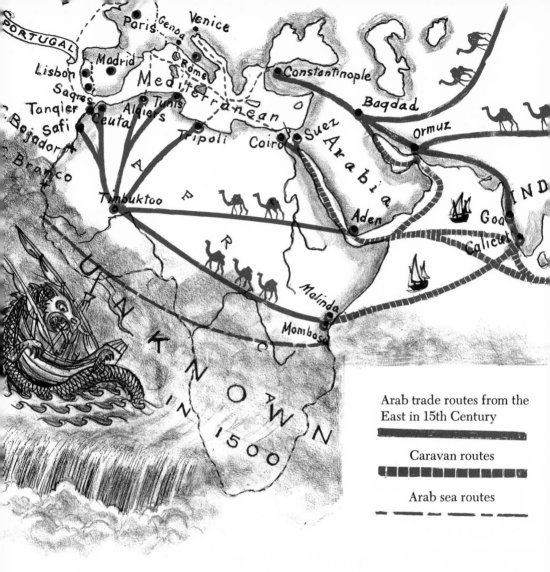

Arab trade routes from the East in 15th Century

Caravan routes

Arab sea routes

would be no profits in a voyage to an uninhabited coast. Captains of the fifteenth century were looking for rich cities where they could trade for gold, jewels, silks and spices and slaves. This brings us to the man whose imagination and stubborn determination overcame all obstacles and won for Portugal a great empire and fabulous riches.

14

Prince Henry and the
Storming of Ceuta

John I, King of Portugal from 1385 to 1433, had preserved the independence of his tiny country by defeating the Castilians at the battle of Aljuberotta in 1385. An uneasy peace existed between Spain and Portugal but this very peace brought about another war.

John I and his Queen Felipa had six children, five boys and one girl. The older sons, Duarte the Crown Prince, Pedro, Henry and John had reached the age of knighthood. In those days the only way a knight could deserve the accolade and win his spurs was by performing some daring feat in combat. The peace with Spain, which surrounded their country, made it impossible for the princes to do battle.

Across the Straits of Gibraltar in African Morocco on a commanding peninsula, stood the rich Moorish city of Ceuta, gateway for the eastern merchandise brought up from India, Africa and Arabia by caravan and for seaborne cargoes from the eastern Mediterranean. If the Portuguese could conquer Ceuta they thought they could control all the trade of North Africa and use the city as a base for later expeditions inland or down the coast. As the Portuguese were very devout Christians the capture of Ceuta would make it possible to convert the Moorish worshipers of Mohammed to Christianity, thus making it a Holy war.

The young princes were all eager to do battle. This would give them a chance to become knights in the only worthwhile way, by distinguishing themselves in combat. They pleaded with their father to give his consent, but the King was reluctant. He pointed out that they would need a great fleet of ships, which did not exist, that such a campaign would require a great deal of money, while his treasury was almost empty, and that if they won the Moors would be sure to avenge their defeat by attacking the southern coast of Portugal. Nevertheless the young princes pleaded so strongly that finally the King gave in. However, he insisted that their only chance to win was to make a surprise attack, so that all their preparations would have to be kept a complete secret. He knew that the building of a great fleet, the casting of cannon, the gathering of men and supplies for an army, would certainly be noticed by the Moors, who still occupied the Spanish province of Granada not far from the Portuguese border.

King John decided to pretend that he was arming against the Dutch, using as an excuse the rough treatment of Portuguese traders in Holland. The King sent an ambassador to the court of Prince William of Holland, to publicly declare war against the Dutch. However, in a private meeting with the Prince, the ambassador revealed King John's real purpose and assured him he had nothing to fear. Meanwhile the Portuguese spread the word that when their fleet was ready it would sail north to do battle against the Dutch.

The nation's resources were all devoted to preparation for war. For three years the shipyards of Lisbon, Oporto and Lagos swarmed with shipwrights and riggers, the tap-tap of calking hammers sounded everywhere, sail lofts and rope walks were busy from dawn to dark. The glare of the furnaces in the cannon foundries turned night into day, while great sheaves of spears, swords and crossbows were hammered out by the armorers.

The King and his advisers desperately needed information about the defences of Ceuta, how the fortifications were laid out, the depth of water in the harbor, and any weaknesses in the walls and towers. Yet they dared not raise the suspicions of the Moors by sending out military scouts as spies. Then luck gave the King an opportunity. The widowed Queen of Sicily sent word that she would like to marry Prince Duarte, the King's heir. The King saw his chance. He would send ambassadors to Sicily to offer the hand of his second son Pedro, instead of the Crown Prince's, knowing that she would refuse to take second best. The ship carrying the ambassadors would cause no suspicion if it put in to Ceuta on its way to Sicily. While at anchor there the ambassadors could use their eyes to good purpose. King John chose a Captain Furtado and the Prior of the Knights Hospitalers as his envoys and fitted out two fast galleys, decorated with banners, oriflammes and silk awnings in the royal colors, gilded and carved in such splendor as had never before been seen.

As planned the ships put in at Ceuta, and while at anchor the two envoys took note of everything they could see without being noticed by the Moors. Then they sailed on to Sicily, where their offer was spurned by the Queen, as had been foreseen. They returned to Lisbon to report.

Captain Furtado told a strange story of meeting an old man at a port near Ceuta, who foretold that King John would successfully storm the city; he assured the King that he would be victorious, but would add nothing more. The Prior too refused to speak until he had been given two bags of sand, half a bushel of beans, some thread and a bowl. The King was angered at their stubbornness but finally ordered servants to bring the Prior what he desired. The old man took the things

into another room and closed the door behind him.
When at last he opened it he showed the King an exact
model of the peninsula on which the city stood. It was
made of sand, with the layout of the city walls marked
out with thread, and gates and buildings shown with

beans. This gave the King all he needed to plan his attack strategy.

The ships of the fleets had now been launched in the different Portuguese harbors. Among the lighter oared vessels were galleys, galeates, tardantes and saetias, while the sailing ships included barcas, carracks, fustas, balenares, pinazas and carabelas, one, two and three-masted vessels, some with lateen sails, others square-rigged, ranging from less than 50 to 100 tons.

Prince Henry, now twenty-one years old, had shown tremendous zeal in the preparations for war. He was given command of the fleet gathered in the harbor of Oporto, while Prince Pedro was put in charge of the Lisbon fleet, under his father, the King. During the King's absence Prince Duarte would rule the country.

As summer approached Prince Henry was ordered to bring his fleet from Oporto to join the ships of Prince Pedro anchored in the Tagus river at Lisbon. The troops and their supplies were loaded aboard and on July 25th, 1415, while thousands of Lisbon people came down to watch, the fleet prepared to leave. A favorable wind from the north was blowing, creaking yards rose, canvas cracked and billowed and sweating seamen manned the windlasses to bring up the dripping anchors. The combined fleet, one of the largest ever seen at that time, headed down the coast before the following breeze, making for the Straits of Gibraltar and the Mediterranean.

There were 59 rowing galleys, 32 biremes and 27 triremes, 63 transports and 120 other vessels. At sunset of July 27th they slowly rounded Cape St. Vincent and came to anchor in the small port of Lagos, 15 miles to the east. Here they took on water and supplies, and the troops were at last told their destination, Ceuta, just across the Straits.

The fleet left Lagos on July 30th, expecting to reach Ceuta and begin the attack in a couple of days, but it became a victim of the fickle master of all sailing ships —the wind. For a whole week the ships lay becalmed, drifting helplessly backward and forward with the tides. The rowing galleys, which could have reached Ceuta, dared not leave the fleet, so they too were helpless.

Food and water were beginning to run low, and to make matters worse, plague appeared aboard the ships and men began to sicken and die. At last the wind picked up and the fleet worked its way painfully into the bay at the foot of the towering rock of Gibraltar.

On August 10th a council of the leaders decided that the fleet would sail that night, to be in position to attack on the 12th. Again lack of wind foiled their plans, and the swift tides of the Straits dispersed the ships as far as sixty miles apart; only the galleys got into position before Ceuta. The fleet became so disorganized that it had to return to the Bay of Gibraltar to make a new start.

This misfortune actually helped the Portuguese in the end. When the Governor of Ceuta saw the first of the galleys appear below his walls he sent for help from the ruler of Fez and from the Berber tribesmen who

21

lived among the hills to the south. However when the fleet became separated and most of the ships disappeared over the horizon, he decided that the attack was to be directed at the citadel of Gibraltar across the Straits and not at Ceuta, so he told his allies to call off their reinforcements.

At last, on August 30th, with the wind at last favorable, the Portuguese fleet spread its canvas and headed out into the Straits. The plan of attack called for Prince Henry with forty or fifty ships to anchor on the eastern side of the Peninsula, while the main fleet headed into Ceuta Bay on the west side. The Portuguese hoped that most of the defenders would man the west walls facing their main fleet, which would permit Prince Henry's force to surprise the lightly held eastern defenses.

All through the night Sala-ben-Sala, the governor of the city ordered lights placed in every window and embrasure of the walls, and stationed men-at-arms along the top, waving their weapons and yelling defiance, to impress the enemy with his alertness.

As dawn drove the mists away, Henry's force prepared to land, awaiting King John's signal to begin the attack. Then a nobleman named Ruy Gonçalves leaped ashore, and Henry, annoyed because he had wanted to be the first man on the beach, waited no longer. He ordered the trumpeters to sound the charge, and led a wave of armed men ashore. As they splashed ashore the gates opened and the Moors poured out. As the Portuguese had hoped, the walls on their side were only

lightly held and the Christians soon drove back the enemy through the gates and entered the city.

Now King John's troops landed and attacked the western side, whose defenders were becoming disorganized by Prince Henry's charge from the rear. The Moors reeled back from the fierce sallies of the Portuguese and soon Sala-ben-Sala, with a few of his officers, their wives and some treasure, fled through a landward gate and took to the hills. By nightfall the citadel, the last Moorish stronghold, fell and Ceuta belonged to the Portuguese, along with its treasures of gold and jewels, rich carpets, rare tapestries, bolts of fine silks and jars of oil and spices.

The Sunday after the battle a sacred Mass was held in a Moorish mosque which had been cleansed and consecrated, while overhead two church bells boomed — bells which long ago had been captured by the Moors from a church in Sines, a small town in the Portuguese province of Algarve.

After the Mass the young princes returned to their apartments, bathed and donned their best armor, polished and gleaming for the occasion, and returned to the Church. They knelt before their father and were awarded the accolade of knighthood they had so nobly won during the fierce battle.

With Ceuta securely in Portuguese hands, King John ordered his fleet to return to Lisbon, leaving a garrison of three thousand men under Count Dom Pedro de Menezes to protect it from recapture by the Moors. When the news of the battle reached Europe the Portuguese were greatly respected by the other nations for their victory over the once invincible Moors, but this was about the only benefit they received from their capture of Ceuta. The Moors stopped sending their caravans of merchandise to the city, and the artisans and traders fled from the city. Ceuta became a ghost town, bringing no profits to the new masters.

The Moors never lost hope of recapturing their port. In 1418, three years after its surrender, Ceuta was so heavily besieged by them that de Menezes had to call for help and Prince Henry was dispatched with a strong fleet to relieve the city. When his sails appeared on the horizon the Moors lost heart and retired into the hills, so Henry found himself with a war fleet and no enemy. At once he thought of attacking Gibraltar, that great rock fortress belonging to the Moors who still owned Granada. With Gibraltar in his hands he could soon overcome Tangier at the mouth of the Straits and thus control all the shipping passing between the Mediterranean and the Atlantic.

He wrote his father, the King, for permission to attack Gibraltar, but King John refused and ordered Henry home. Henry was never happy in Lisbon, so, as Duke of Viseu, he decided to make his home in the southernmost Portuguese province of Algarve. Here he would be nearer to Ceuta of which he was absentee governor, and also he would be nearer the African coast, whose mysteries were beginning to challenge his imagination.

He chose as the site for his new palace and fortress

the bold rocky, spray-swept headland of Sagres at the southwest corner of Portugal. It jutted out into the Atlantic, swept by the great waves which rolled in from the fearsome, mysterious regions to the south and west. Here, over the years he built his Vila do Infante, the City of the Prince, overlooked by the grim gray palace rising from the heights of the bleak, rocky point. Henry invited to his palace the learned men of all the world who were offered bountiful hospitality and large rewards for sharing their knowledge. Here were gathered the foremost cartographers, geographers, navigators, mathematicians, astronomers, world travelers, ship designers, and even Moors and Africans who might tell him something about the interior of the great continent to the south. He listened with close attention to all they could tell and employed their skills to help in his plans to discover what lay beyond the horizon.

Prince Henry, The Navigator

Prince Henry was especially eager to learn everything he could about the new science of navigation, so that the captains of his ships could find their positions on the trackless oceans. In the fifteenth century a ship's navigator had the benefit of only a few instruments.

First was the compass, already used by the Chinese and the Phoenicians for centuries. It was a magnetized steel needle, swinging on a pivot, which always pointed north and thus told the mariner in which direction he was sailing. It was not perfectly true because it pointed not to true North, but to magnetic North, which varied slightly from year to year, and so caused an error called variation. The needle could also be pulled to one side or the other by the attraction of anything made of iron aboard the ship itself, causing an error called deviation. Variation was marked on the charts by the astronomers' calculations, and deviation was corrected by placing magnets at either side of the compass.

Second was the ship's log, so called because in its earliest form it was really a small log. Tied to a cord the log was heaved overboard at the bow, while the ship was under way, and the time it took to reach the stern was recorded with an hour glass. Since the ship's length was known, her speed over the water could be worked out.

The third was an instrument by which the altitude or distance above the horizon of the sun or other heavenly body could be measured in degrees. Then, from tables worked out by the astronomers, a navigator could find his latitude, the distance his ship lay north or south of the equator. The earliest instrument for such observations, called an astrolabe, was a brass ring marked in degrees, with a pivoted crossbar with a peephole at each end. The observer held up the astrolabe by a small ring at the top and sighted the sun through the peepholes, then read the degrees as shown by the crossbar. It was very hard to take an accurate bearing with the astrolabe on a pitching, rolling deck, so if the ship lay near the coast mariners often anchored and went ashore in a small boat to take a bearing with the astrolabe on firm ground.

A later instrument, used by Henry's navigators, by which bearings could be taken from the deck, was the cross-staff, a long straight piece of wood, marked out in degrees, with a peephole at one end. Another piece, at right angles, could be slid along the first. The navigator aimed the long staff at the horizon, then moved the cross-staff along it until its top lined up between the lower edge of the sun and the peephole at the end of the staff. He then read the degrees shown where the two staffs crossed, which gave him the angle in degrees between the sun and the horizon. By subtracting this sum from 90 degrees, the right angle formed between the horizon and the zenith (the point directly over-head) he found how many degrees his ship lay from the latitude over which the sun was passing on that particular day. This was still of no help unless he knew what the sun's latitude was on that day. Prince Henry set up an observatory in his palace and set his astronomers to work observing the course of the sun all through the year so that they could compile a set of tables which showed the sun's declination, or distance north or south of the Equator as it crossed from east to west on any given day in the year. With these tables the navigator could add to or subtract from (depending on the season of the year) the sum he had obtained by the

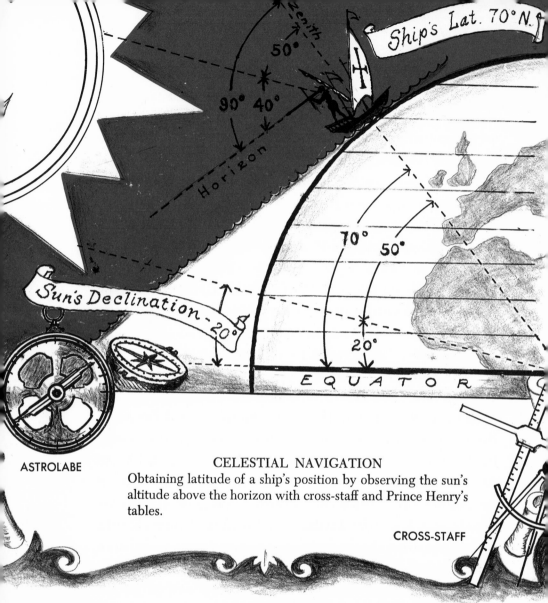

Ship's Lat. 70° N.

Zenith

50°

90° 40°

Horizon

70° 50°

20°

Sun's Declination - 20°

E Q U A T O R

ASTROLABE

CELESTIAL NAVIGATION
Obtaining latitude of a ship's position by observing the sun's
altitude above the horizon with cross-staff and Prince Henry's
tables.

CROSS-STAFF

cross-staff, the sun's declination for that day, and obtain
his latitude, or distance his ship lay from the equator.
Longitude, the ship's position east or west of a line
called 0 longitude, would have to wait for the inven-

tion of an accurate chronometer or clock, which was not achieved until the mid-eighteenth century. Still, the fifteenth century navigator, by sailing to the parallel of latitude on which his destination lay according to the chart, then sailing along that parallel on a compass bearing, could know, by dead reckoning (estimating his distance covered by the speed shown by the log) when he was near his goal, and could usually soon sight it. The diagram illustrated here showing the method of taking a noon sight, explains celestial navigation more clearly than words. For the Portuguese captains, sailing southward along a very long coastline, latitude was much more important than longitude.

With these three instruments as his only guide, the Portuguese navigator set out on long journeys out of sight of land for many weeks, over completely unexplored waters. He had no charts to show him coast lines, islands or treacherous reefs or to indicate depths of the waters. There were no tide and current tables to warn him of tide rips or strong currents to set him off his course. Only after the earliest navigators had made charts, marking the latitudes of islands, river mouths and capes, and their approximate distances, and tested the strength and direction of the currents they encountered, did later navigators have any idea of what lay ahead.

Ships of the Portuguese Explorers

For hundreds of years the Phoenicians, the Egyptians, the Greeks and Romans and later the Venetians and Genoese had plied the Mediterranean and even ventured beyond the Straits of Gibraltar into the stormy Atlantic as far as England and Holland. Before the fifteenth century ships had stayed mainly in the Mediterranean, where, although the strong winds, the levanter or the sirocco, could stir up fierce storms, the weather was never as terrible as a full Atlantic gale.

The earliest ships were undecked open craft, with oars and sometimes with a square sail set on a single mast, called galleys. Most war vessels were galleys because they had to be fast and maneuverable, while merchant ships which had to have roomy holds to carry a lot of merchandise, were rigged with several masts and larger sails to move them. Their bluff-bowed, wide-beamed hulls were too heavy to be propelled by oars.

Sails were either suspended from yards which crossed the masts at right angles and were called square sails, or from very long yards which crossed the mast at a steep angle, with the foot of the sail at the deck and the head far above the mast. These were called lateen sails. Some ships designed for long open ocean voyages carried three or even four masts, usually with the foremast square-rigged and the others lateen. Seamen found that ships entirely lateen-rigged did not handle well over the larger waves of the open ocean; the square foresail helped steady them. On long voyages crews and cargoes needed better protection than an open hull could give, so the shipyards began building half-decked hulls, and finally completely decked-over vessels, with fore and sterncastles rising high above the main deck or waist. Ships were still so slow sailing that they needed a raised stern to keep the following waves from overtaking the vessel and sweeping the decks under tons of water.

The earliest Portuguese explorers set forth in small, open-decked barcas and rowing galleys but they soon found that larger ships with better shelter would be needed. The seas on the open Atlantic were often too high to permit the use of oars, so they soon gave up

The BÉRRIO

BARCA

CARRACK

CARAVELO REDON.

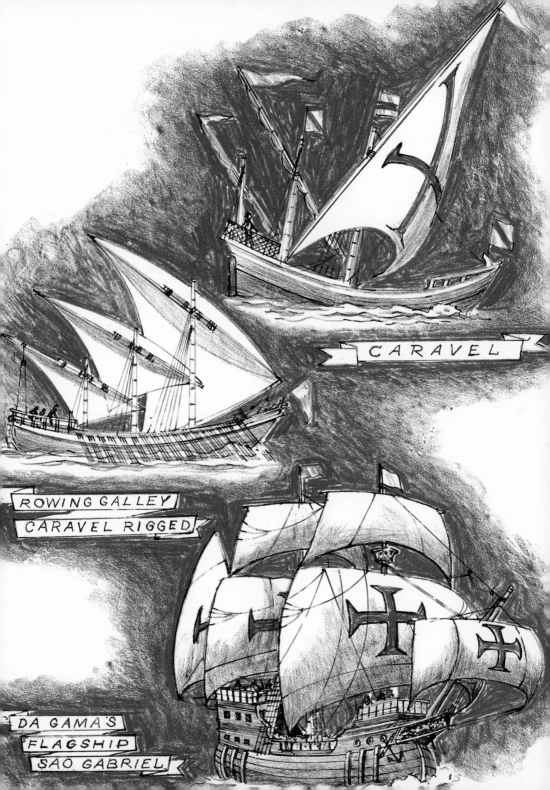

CARAVEL

ROWING GALLEY
CARAVEL RIGGED

DA GAMA'S
FLAGSHIP
SAO GABRIEL

using rowing galleys. The larger carracks and caravels of from 60 to 90 feet, with a beam of from 20 to 30 feet, were much more successful, especially caravels re-rigged with square sails on one or two of the masts, called caraveles redonda. Still later, in the seventeenth century the galleon appeared and became the type most commonly used for long voyages. Columbus always felt that smaller, shallow-draft ships were most useful for exploration, because they could operate in shoal water and in narrow channels. Because the Portuguese were very religious and always considered the conversion of the natives an important part of a voyage of exploration, the sails of their ships were always emblazoned with huge red crosses, by which they could easily be identified.

Even the best fifteenth century ships were cranky and clumsy and could only make progress with the wind from astern or abeam; with the wind from ahead their tacking ability was almost nil. Storms knocked them about unmercifully and did so much damage that they usually had to limp into some port to repair damages and refit. After a few weeks at sea they often sprang so many leaks that the pumps had to be kept going constantly. Without copper sheathing their bottoms soon gathered heavy growths of weeds as well as worms that riddled the planks and rotted the hulls. Yet in these badly-built little ships Portuguese captains made voyages of thousands of miles, opened up two continents and discovered a new route to India and China.

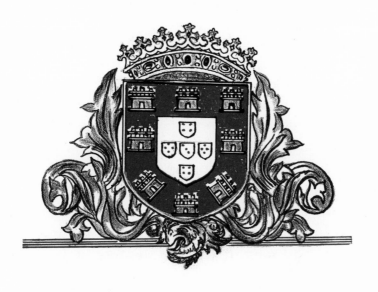

Prince Henry's First Expeditions

Prince Henry was now twenty-five years old. He had finished building his palace and brought together learned men to train his captains so that they could navigate his ships to the places he wanted them to go. His governorship of Ceuta now gave him little concern. But that ever-present mystery of the empty horizon gave him no peace — lying always before his eyes as he stood on the wind-swept ramparts of his castle atop the cliffs at Sagres.

One day there came to his castle two of his young squires, João Gonçalves Zarco and Tristão Vaz Teixiera, who were restless, bored and short of money. They begged Prince Henry to give them a chance for adventure; they were eager to go on any mission he might have in mind. Their eagerness pleased Henry and fitted in with an expedition he was planning. He fitted out two tiny barcas, well under 100 tons, and gave their command to Zarco and Teixiera, with instructions to head southward as far as they could go and report what they had seen. It was the summer of 1420 when the two frail barcas put out from the harbor of Palos, passed the Straits of Gibraltar and the safe shipping routes to plunge into the perilous unknown seas off the coast of Africa.

How far south they voyaged was never discovered, but when they returned to Palos in their battered little ships they told Henry of having weathered a terrible storm by discovering a bare little island with rocky peaks where a sandy bay sheltered them while they made much-needed repairs. They called the island Porto Santo, but they lingered only long enough to finish the repairs; after three days they set sail for Portugal. Prince Henry was delighted to learn of the island; he was eager to establish ports of call southward, and at once ordered the two explorers back to establish a colony. Henry knew that a group of small islands called the Canaries had long ago been discovered by the Spanish, who now claimed them although they had never settled them. But whether Porto Santo belonged to the Canaries no one was sure. As it turned out Porto Santo and the larger nearby island Madeira, which they discovered next, were well north of the Canaries and so could not legally be claimed by the King of Spain.

Zarco and Teixiera, this time accompanied by another squire named Perestrello, cheerfully set out again in three little ships, with a group of settlers, seeds and plants and enough supplies for a long stay. On leaving, a friend gave Perestrello a doe rabbit in a cage, and she produced a litter of young during the voyage.

The colonists landed on Porto Santo and soon had shelters built and crops planted. The climate was good and the ground so fertile that the colony would have flourished except for one thing — Perestrello's rabbits. He had let them out of their cage when they landed, and they found the island a rabbit heaven, with plenty of food and no predatory animals to keep down their numbers. They multiplied so fast that they ate the colonists' crops as soon as they showed above ground. After a two years' struggle the rabbits won, and the discouraged colonists gave up and returned to Portugal.

Henry received them without reproach and urged them to try again and to seek more islands where they might have better luck. Zarco had told him of a strange cloud to the south which never seemed to move, and the Prince felt sure that this indicated land below it;

let the explorers sail toward that cloud and find out, he urged.

In June 1424 they made their third voyage to Porto Santo, where they found the rabbits still in command, and where that low-hanging cloud still lay motionless along the southern horizon. On Sunday July 1st, they laid a course for it, and presently they could hear the crashing of surf against forbidding cliffs dimly seen through clouds. At last the warm sun melted the fog and revealed a lovely green island with thickly wooded mountain slopes rising steeply and sheltering a bay with beautiful white sandy beaches which the ships entered to anchor.

The people rowed ashore. Clear streams splashed and gurgled out of the hills, but everywhere the trees grew so thickly they found it hard to make their way inland. Under the green canopy arching overhead they sank deeply into a thick carpet of leaves piled up through the centuries. They found no animals, insects or snakes; all that broke the silence was the twittering of countless birds. To some of the people it was the Island of Birds but the leader named their discovery Madeira, meaning "heavily wooded" and claimed it for Portugal.

The only sign of human life was a ruined, weather-beaten shack beside the bay, where a wooden cross had been erected bearing this carved inscription in Latin: "Here came Machin, an Englishman, driven by the tempest, and here lies buried Anna d'Arfet, a woman who was with him." Of Machin and his lady, of who buried them and set up the cross, nothing but vague rumors were ever discovered. Certainly the Portuguese were now the only inhabitants. They gathered plants, herbs, branches of trees and earth to show Prince Henry as he had asked, and returned to Portugal with the news of their discovery.

During their absence Henry had sent out an expedition under Dom Fernando de Castro to try to set up a base on Grand Canary, the largest of the Canary Islands, but Castro found the natives too numerous and too fierce for him to risk a landing. After his return to Lisbon the King of Castile learned of his expedition and objected strongly to Portuguese encroachment, even though he had not as yet established any settlements on the Canaries.

The return of the ships from Madeira, with their good news, was greeted with great joy by the Prince; at last, it seemed, he had a promising colony which might even bring some return on the money he had laid out for his expeditions. Prince Henry divided the administration of the island between Zarco and Teixiera, who volunteered to bring out their families and settle on Madeira. Inmates of the State prisons who looked promising were given their freedom in exchange for settling on the island, and so three ships were loaded with colonists, tools, cattle, pigs, sheep and fowls as well as seeds, plants and fruit trees. Prince Henry saw them off with high hopes that this colony would succeed.

All too soon one of the ships returned with terrible

news; the whole island was on fire! To prepare the land for planting the colonists had to get rid of the mountains of dead leaves which covered the ground, so they set fire to them, and soon the fire got out of control, spread to the virgin forest and roared across the whole island. The settlers had to retreat to the water's edge when the wind sent the flames in their direction, and there they crouched covered with ashes and choking on the smoke-filled air, barely existing on shellfish until the worst was over. Still they stuck it out, waiting for the fires to die and let them go to work. In the Funchal valley it was reported that underground fires burned for seven years, but where the ground had cooled elsewhere the ground was so rich that anything would grow.

The Prince sent more tools, seeds and livestock, and sent out more settlers to work the land. He was sure that sugar and grapes would thrive, so he imported sugar cane from Sicily and malmsey grape vines from Cyprus, hiring expert sugar workers and vintners to raise them. Soon Madeira wine became famous all over the world, and Madeira honey, wax and sugar were of the finest quality. Cattle, sheep and goats as well as fowls grew fat and sleek. There was soon a large lumber trade in the fine timber spared by the fires. The prosperity of Madeira encouraged Prince Henry to take the next step in his great plan.

Prince Henry still patiently urged his captains to sail farther south, but they all found excuses for not venturing beyond Cape Bojador. They couldn't see any

profit in sailing southward along a coast behind
which lay only the vast desert, silent and unpopu-
lated. They much preferred raiding Moorish ports and

looting their ships in the Mediterranean. Although some of the captains were not taken in by the wild stories of boiling seas and the danger of falling over the edge of the world, they did know that the strong prevailing winds were from the northeast and that a powerful southerly current flowed between Madeira and the coast. This was fine for a vessel bound south, but no ship could beat back north again. The only way to return would be to sail far enough west and get beyond those northeast trade winds, making a wide circle to return home. Nobody at that time knew anything about what the weather was like toward mid-Atlantic, so Henry sent out ship after ship to study the winds and currents there. Some of the reports they brought back made him suspect that there might be islands far out at sea, due west of Portugal.

The Prince called in an old friend, an expert seaman and a veteran of the fighting in North Africa, named Goncalo Velho Cabral, and asked him to try to find those islands. Cabral sailed forth into the setting sun and presently discovered islands where he expected to find them, but they turned out to be only low rocky reefs, washed over by mountainous surf, on which no landings could be made. Cabral sailed home and reported his find to the Prince, who thanked him for his efforts but urged him to try again; there were surely more islands somewhere about and Cabral could find them.

Again the brave captain set out, and this time, 1432, found Santa Maria, one of the Azores, a pleasant wooded well-watered island entirely without animal life; only birds of many kinds flitted through the silent forest or swooped above the creaming surf along the white beaches. The Azores were so far out to sea, almost a thousand miles, and so isolated that Henry decided not to colonize them at once; there was little fear of some other country claiming them. Instead he ordered Cabral to stock Santa Maria with livestock and fowls and let them multiply, so that the island would become a food supply base for his ships returning from African voyages, and for future colonists. Not until 1439 was Cabral ordered to recruit colonists and settle the Azores.

In August 1433 old King John (João), now in his 70's, died and his eldest son, Duarte, ascended the throne amid great pageantry and ceremony. Prince Henry came up to Lisbon from his bleak palace at Sagres for the festivities but soon returned to his endless studies of the sea, the winds and the stars.

By this time he was certain that a southward passage beyond that terrifying Cape Bojador was perfectly safe and the return to Portugal quite possible. The problem was to convince the superstitious mariners, for even though a captain was willing, his crew might mutiny and force him to turn back. The Prince commissioned his squire Gil Eanes of Lagos to break that wall of fear which held back seamen and drive boldly into the mysterious, terrifying seas beyond the Cape. Alas, the same terrors which held back other captains overcame Gil Eanes and he returned without even passing beyond the Canaries, which had been discovered a hundred years before.

A year later, in 1434, the Prince ordered Gil Eanes to try again, telling him he should be ashamed to believe the wild rumors of ignorant seamen; all he asked was that Eanes should sail beyond Bojador. Gil Eanes promised that this time nothing could stop him, and he held his course boldly past the dread Cape, while his fearful crew gave themselves up for lost. With the Cape far astern, Gil Eanes and his men discovered that the sea looked no different from the water to the north; there were no boiling waves teeming with monsters, but only placid wavelets breaking on a sandy, barren, treeless shore where nothing moved. Eanes had himself rowed ashore, where he picked some dry herbs and

flowers, all that he could find to bring back to the Prince to prove he had landed. The only signs of life were some camel tracks almost drifted over in the sand.

When the ship arrived in Sagres and Gil Eanes showed the Prince the bedraggled flowers and plants, all he had for his pains, the Prince was far from displeased. Gil Eanes had brought him something far more valuable; he had proved that the tales of the horrors beyond Cape Bojador were untrue, and from the camel tracks the men had seen, that people lived in the desert. Now his captains could sail southward with easy minds and he could get on with his grand plan.

A new expedition was fitted out and Gil Eanes sailed again with instructions to steer ever southward. Day after day the little vessels skirted the coastal desert,

shimmering in the brilliant tropical sun. It was so flat that the steersmen often found it difficult to see where the water ended and the land began. When they had gone about 120 leagues (a league was about 5 miles) beyond Cape Bojador they came to a deep bay which they thought was the mouth of a great river, and so named it Rio de Ouro, or River of Gold. Here they anchored and Gil Eanes sent ashore two boys with horses, to ride inland to see what they could find. The boys trotted across the sand and soon came upon a group of nineteen natives armed with spears, whom the boys promptly attacked, hoping to capture one or two. Although the natives were panic-stricken by the horses which they had never seen before, they defended themselves so fiercely that the boys had to return empty-handed. Next day more of the crew went ashore, but the natives had fled and they had to be content to kill some sea lions which lived in great numbers at the mouth of the bay, and bring back their skins and some beautifully woven-bark fish nets. The expedition returned to Portugal to report to Prince Henry; it would be the last for years, because tragic new activities in Portugal now kept the Prince so occupied that for a long time he had no time for exploration.

Old King John on his deathbed had begged his sons to continue their war against the Moorish unbelievers and bring the Christian faith to North Africa. The Princes decided that the time was ripe to carry out their father's wishes. The first step was to attack and capture the city of Tangier on the African side of the

Straits of Gibraltar, not far west of their own strong-hold of Ceuta. Ceuta was isolated by a ring of Moorish fortifications which blocked any chance of Portuguese trading with African caravans. The capture of Tangier would free it and put all of northern Morocco in Por-tuguese hands. This would permit trade with the Arabs and allow the Portuguese to begin converting the Afri-can tribes to the south. Perhaps they might even link up with Prester John, believed to be King of a Christian Empire somewhere to the southeast.

This time the triumph of Ceuta was not repeated; the Moors were ready for the Portuguese army under Prince Henry. His troops were routed and forced to surrender. The Moors demanded as a price for freeing the army that Ceuta be turned over to them. To make sure that their terms be met, they took as a hostage Henry's younger brother, Ferdinand. Because terms could not be agreed upon, Ferdinand died after years of brutal captivity, a blow from which Henry never recovered.

Then another tragedy fell upon the small country. King Duarte died after only a short reign, and his small son became King Afonso V. After much bickering be-tween the Queen's friends and the uncles of the new King, Prince Pedro, Henry's elder brother, was named Regent until Afonso should reach the age of twelve. Luckily Pedro was eager for Henry to continue his ex-plorations and backed him fully.

After five long years of delay, Prince Henry was again ready. He fitted out two small ships, giving command of the first to a young squire named Antão Gonçalves, with instructions to bring back oil and sea lions' skins from the Rio Ouro. The second ship was put under command of a bright knight named Nuno Tristão, and he was told to pass the most southerly point yet reached and to sail as far beyond it as he could. His vessel was a new type. Instead of the usual barco, a lateen-rigged caravel, of only fifty tons, proved to be swift and easily handled. She was able to make headway against the wind far better than any other ships of the time, and was also the first of Henry's ships to be armed with bombards, or cannon. For a century the Portuguese caravel dominated the sea routes.

Tristão took with him a Bedouin, or desert Arab, who might be able to translate the words of any natives they met on the voyage. When the two ships met at the Rio Ouro, Gonçalves had already captured a Negro man and an old woman, but even the Bedouin could not understand their language. So the two captains led a joint expedition ashore by night, surprised and attacked a nomad camp of Arabs and captured ten prisoners, who were taken aboard a ship. One of the prisoners, evidently a chieftain named Adahu, was so respected by the Portuguese that they treated him as a knight.

When the time came for them to part company, Nuno knighted his young companion Gonçalves, who then sailed off to Portugal with the prisoners, among them the noble Adahu, and a load of sea lions' skins. When they landed at Lisbon the captured Africans

created great excitement and large crowds gathered to look at them. They were well treated, taught some Portuguese, and learned about Christianity.

Meanwhile Tristão, although a thousand miles from home, beached his caravel, careened her and put his men to scraping weed and barnacles from her bottom, calking open seams and renewing weakened rigging, in preparation for pushing farther south. Obeying his instructions he sailed far beyond Rio de Ouro for one hundred and fifty leagues, to another Cape which he named Branco, or White Cape, where he found the shore to be barren, sandy desert, empty and silent. Here he was forced to turn back because his provisions were running out.

At Sagres, Prince Henry had been hearing, through interpreters, fascinating tales about Africa from the Chieftain Adahu — stories which made him more determined than ever to explore the mysterious continent. He learned about the great desert port of Timbuktoo, far up the Niger River, where many of the ancient caravan routes converged, where long processions of camels laden with gold, spices, silks and salt, padded silently into the city from the vast Sahara which stretched across Africa from the Atlantic to the Red Sea.

Adahu related than no one man had ever followed a cargo of gold from its origin far to the east until it reached Timbuktoo, or laid eyes on the caravaneers who carried it over the previous stage. At the edge of the desert, where gold from the east was bartered for salt from the ocean, the salt traders piled their salt in a certain place, adding more each day until the men from the east considered the pile large enough. Then during the night the salt pile disappeared and the gold lay in its place.

Henry heard of strange naked black people living in green jungles south of the great desert, of strange beasts, fierce lions and ponderous elephants with ivory tusks longer than a man is tall. They were killed by native bowmen with tiny poisoned arrows. At last, having revealed what he knew, Adahu was beginning to tire of his life so far from home and asked to be sent back, offering a ransom of five or six fine Negro slaves for his release. Gonçalves agreed to sail back to Rio de Ouro with Adahu and the other Arab prisoners he had taken. There he obtained a hundred Negroes in exchange for the Arabs as well as some gold dust and a number of ostrich eggs.

Suddenly people began to be interested in Prince Henry's expeditions; those black captives his captains brought back were becoming valuable merchandise — as slaves. This was the beginning of the slave trade, in which the rest of Europe and American colonies shared.

The Portuguese eased their consciences by converting their slaves to Christianity and thus saving their souls, which to them seemed a fair exchange for the use of their bodies. They treated their slaves well, gave them the same rights as the whites, fed and clothed them well. Later, in other lands the black slaves were treated harshly.

Up to this time all the Portuguese expeditions had

reported endless burning sandy wastes when they went ashore. Now, one Denis Diaz, putting out from Lagos, determined not to go ashore until he had passed beyond the desert beaches and reached the green land described by Negro captives.

Cape Branco had long since dropped below the horizon astern when at last Diaz smelled the fragrance of lush vegetation on the breeze, and presently saw palm trees outlined against the sky along a promontory he named Cape Verde, the Green Cape. His caravel anchored off a rocky island covered by gigantic trees, inhabited only by herds of wild goats. The arrival of their giant "white bird" filled the native blacks with wonder and curiosity; they had watched the ship's approach from the mainland, and presently their canoes were approaching closer. Diaz's men were able to capture four of them and take them back to Portugal with the glad news of the discovery of a green, fertile, populated coast at last.

By this time other enterprising men were fitting out ships using their own money and sending them forth to explore this newly found coast of Guinea and bring back whatever treasure trove they could find. Alvaro Fernandes, nephew of João Zarco, the discoverer of Madeira, discovered the mouth of a mighty river, which he believed to be a branch of the Nile, but was later found to be a separate stream later called the Senegal.

This new country revealed wonder after wonder to the Portuguese mariners. Gigantic trees, fantastic plants and exotic fruits and flowers dazzled their eyes.

But they soon found that the black men who lived in these jungles were much more ferocious than the desert dwellers to the north. Often all that saved the lives of the mariners from the fierce attacks of bowmen and spearmen were the great stones and loads of sharp scrap iron hurled at their canoes by the ships' bombards.

Sometimes those encounters ended tragically. Nuno Tristão, commanding an expedition sailed his caravel into the mouth of an unknown river some sixty leagues beyond Cape Verde and anchored. In two of the small boats he and his crew rowed upstream where the trees formed a dark twilit canopy overhead and the water gurgled between banks which were an impenetrable tangle of mangrove roots.

Suddenly the dim green silence was broken by shrill cries, the splashing of many paddles and the boats were surrounded by twelve canoes filled with savages armed with bows. Flight after flight of flimsy reed arrows whispered down on them, so tiny that they only pricked the skin like insects, but each prick meant certain death, for every arrowhead was coated with deadly poison.

The two boats were hastily rowed back to their ship by the panic-stricken sailors hotly pursued by the Africans in their canoes. Two of the white men were already dead when the crew climbed painfully aboard and the rest were so weakened that they could barely hoist a sail. When they tried to raise the anchor new flights of arrows drove them from the capstan, so they had to cut the cable. The ship drifted slowly seaward

while one by one the men died on the deck; only a young ship's clerk, two little pages and one seaman remained unwounded.

The seaman knew nothing of navigation, all he could do was handle sheets and halliards, so the young clerk, who had watched the officers navigate, set a course as well as he could and hoped for the best. After eight weeks of anxious sailing without sighting any land or another sail, they finally spied a dim blue coastline, which turned out to be Portugal!

When Prince Henry heard the tales of the savage native attacks, instead of sending a strong military force to punish them, as most commanders of that day would have done, he ordered his captains to do their best to trade peacefully with all the tribes they met along the coast. His one wish was to keep on friendly terms with the natives so that his ships might anchor safely in all the West African harbors and be able to barter for food and trade goods in peace.

In the 1450's Diogo Gomes commanded an expedition of three ships which sailed beyond the southernmost latitude yet reached. When strong currents swept them close to shore natives in canoes paddled out to meet them in friendship, offering to barter silk and cotton cloth, ivory and malagueta peppers in their pods. But the ships' anchors began to drag because of the heavy surf, and they had to put out to sea quickly. Anchored again farther south at a Cape which was studded with broken palms, they came ashore at the edge of a vast grassy pasture where they reported see-

ing at least five thousand antelopes grazing fearlessly. They were filled with excitement at the sight of three elephants and two of their young lumbering out of the underbrush. On the way to the beach they also saw crocodiles lurking in the mud.

Presently they reached the mouth of the river Gambia, and sailed far upstream, seeking a city called Cantor, which natives had described to them. There they were told about a great city farther inland, called Kuka, which was fortified by high brick walls, where great caravans gathered, heading for Carthage, Tunis,

Fez and Cairo, bearing rich loads of gold, spices, ivory and silks from Saracen lands.

On their way back to the river mouth they visited a chief named Batimansa, who ruled the land on the left bank of the Gambia, rich in gold mines, with whom Gomes struck up a friendship. Next they met the chief of Alcuzet, who sent Gomes gifts of parrots, leopard skins and elephants' tusks, one so large it took four men to carry it. The chief gave a feast of elephant meat, which the Portuguese considered tough and tasteless, but Gomes had one of the elephants' feet salted down to take back to Prince Henry, who would want to know about everything. When Gomes sailed away from the Gambia he took with him a present from the chief. It was the anchor of Nuno Tristão's caravel which the crew had been unable to raise during that fateful attack years before.

It was probably on this voyage that Gomes discovered the bleak barren Cape Verde Islands, about two hundred miles off the mouth of the Gambia, somewhere between 1457 and 1462. Gomes' expedition was the last sent out by Prince Henry, who died in 1460.

Henry had spent the last years of his life in his lonely windswept castle, a solitary man wrapped in dreams of discovery. Forty years had elapsed since he had sent out his first small barcos; during this time his captains had explored the western coast of Africa almost to the Equator, had discovered all the islands off Portugal, the currents of the open Atlantic, and the African coast. He had made far-reaching studies of the winds and developed the science of navigation, which would be of immense help to later seafarers.

The captains of his last voyages had reported that the coast seemed to be turning eastward, so he had high hopes that at last the tip of Africa had been reached and they could now lay a direct course for India. One look at the map shows how far away they still were from their goal; that triumph would only be achieved by succeeding explorers under other patrons. But the greatest glory belongs to Henry the Navigator.

After Henry's death in 1460, King Afonso became responsible for encouraging further exploration down the African coast. While he favored it, he was far from being as dedicated as Prince Henry. The King leased out the Guinea coast to Fernão Gomes for a rental of 200,000 reis a year, and the promise that he would explore the coast for five hundred leagues beyond the farthest Portuguese outpost.

Gomes carried out his contract vigorously, making a profit over his payments to the Crown by selling gold dust, slaves, ivory and peppers he had bartered for along the coast. His ships followed the coast which turned sharply eastward until they reached an island in the Gulf of Guinea named Fernando Po after its discoverer. There they found that the coast turned southward again. Presently they crossed the Equator and noticed that Polaris, the North Star, by which navigators always guided themselves at night, was dropping below the northern horizon, while strange new galaxies were appearing over the southern skyline. They ranged almost as far south as the mouth of the Congo River, and landed to set up a cross before turning their bows toward Lisbon.

King Afonso died in 1481 and Prince John became King. He was much more ambitious than his father, and he shared Prince Henry's enthusiasm for finding a sea route to India. He soon took back the Guinea concession from Gomes and sent out his own ships to continue the exploration. To make his claims on newly discovered lands more permanent he ordered a number of marble pillars, called padroes, to be carved with the arms of Portugal and surmounted by stone crosses. One of these pillars was to be placed at each important landing place with the King's name, the name of the

NORTH
AMERICA
Treaty of Tordesillas
Spanish
Portuguese
A
T
L
A
N
T
I
C
O
C
E
A
N
PORTUGAL
Azores
Lisbon
Spain
Sagres
Europe
Rome
Tunis
Ceuta
Tangier
Saffi
C. Bojador
Madeira
Canary Is.
A
F
Timbuktoo
Niger R.
Cape Verde Is.
Congo R.
Ascension I.
St. Helena
SOUTH AMERICA
Bahia
BRAZIL
Rio de Janeiro
Cape of Good Hope

The
Portuguese
Explorations
16th Century

stantinople

Ormuz

Aden

Goa
Calicut

CHINA

Macao

JAPAN

Portuguese

Spanish

SPICE IS.
(Moluccas)

Malacca

Sumatra

Borneo

Java

INDIAN

OCEAN

AUSTRALIA

captain who discovered it, and the date carved below the royal arms.

In 1482 the King sent Diogo Cao on a voyage along the coast to set up these padroes at all Portuguese outposts already discovered. Afterward Cao crossed the Equator and continued southward out of sight of land, until one day, a crew member hauling up a bucket of water from over the side, discovered that the water was fresh! This could only mean that some great river was pouring its fresh waters into the ocean. Cao changed his course to the east and presently entered the mouth of the Congo, the second largest river in Africa, after the Nile. Cao named it the Zaire which Portuguese still call it.

The peaceful Negroes he met ashore told him that they were subjects of a great King named Mani Congo, who lived upriver. Cao sent some of his crew to greet the King, give him presents and try to persuade him to become a Christian, while he sailed still farther south. After reaching Cape St. Mary in Angola, at 10 degrees south of the Equator, he planted one of the padroes and returned to the Congo to find that his men had not returned. He took several hostages, promising to return them later, and sailed back to Portugal. True to his promise Cao returned to the Congo with his captives, in 1484, where he was joyfully received by King Mani, who promised to become a Christian.

King John was by now fairly certain that one of his captains would soon be rounding the tip of Africa and entering the Indian Ocean, and he was eager to learn

what they might find there. He therefore sent out two
men named Paiva and Covilha, who spoke Arabic, as
scouts. One was to go to India and the other to find
Prester John, the Christian king who was said to live in
Abyssinia (Ethiopia). They went by way of Italy and
Egypt, thence down the Red Sea, where they sepa-
rated, Paiva to enter Ethiopia and Covilha to cross the
Indian Ocean to Hindustan.

Covilha visited all the great Indian cities on the

west coast, taking note of everything he saw, and even sailed down the East African coast in Arabian ships as far south as Sofala, opposite the great island of Madagascar. When he returned to Cairo he wrote a long letter to the King, describing all he had seen and sent it to Lisbon by a Portuguese merchant he met in Cairo. He himself then headed back to Ethiopia to find Prester John, since he had learned that his companion Paiva had died, and there he disappeared from history for many years.

When King John received Covilha's letter, this, along with the reports of his navigators along the west coast, gave him a pretty good idea of the geography of that great continent Africa. If you look at the map you can see that all that was left unexplored was the shore line from Cape St. Mary in Angola, on the west coast, around the Cape of Good Hope to Sofala on the east. Once this was explored the way to India would be clear.

The King, determined to finish the task, chose a fine navigator and seaman, Bartolomeo Diaz, to head an expedition of three ships to carry his flag to the Indian Ocean. They set out in August, 1486, and sailed steadily southward, passing the point where Cao had set up his last pillar. Now they encountered a great storm from the northwest which forced them to close-reef their sails and run before a mighty wind for thirteen days. When at last the storm blew itself out Diaz headed eastward again in the direction he thought the coast should be. Day after day they ploughed steadily southeast without sighting land, while the weather grew steadily colder. At last Diaz realized that they must have rounded the tip of Africa and that the coast was north of them rather than east. He altered his course and sure enough, after several days lookouts reported land to the north. Diaz landed at Mossel Bay, in South Africa, where he saw herds of cattle, some of which he bought for beef from the herdsmen. As he sailed on he discovered that the coastline was turning north, which convinced him that his ships were entering the Indian Ocean.

Diaz wanted to sail on, and might soon have reached Sofala, which Covilha, sailing from India had already attained, thus completing the circuit of Africa, but his crew rebelled. They were many long months and thousands of miles away from Lisbon, food was running low and the ships were badly in need of refitting; they demanded that Diaz head for home. He asked for only

two days more, which brought them to the Great Fish River. Here he set up a pillar at what is now Algoa Bay and headed for home, passing a cape which he had missed outward bound in the storm. He named it Cape of Storms, but the King, fearing such a name would discourage navigators, renamed it Cape of Good Hope.

One would expect that after the wonderful news of the actual rounding of the Cape the King would have dispatched new expeditions at once; actually it was ten years before the next one, under Vasco da Gama, sailed southward. At that time John had much to keep him busy at home. Diaz had returned with the advice that a different type of ship from the caravels then in use would be needed for making the enormously long voyages between Portugal and India. The King put Diaz in charge of designing and building larger, beamier vessels with high poops and forecastles, but it would take years to complete them.

While the Portuguese were doggedly extending their explorations down the west coast of Africa to develop a sea route to India, a young red-haired Genoese named Christopher Columbus left Genoa for Lisbon, to learn all he could about navigation, geography and seamanship in the country of the foremost sailors. He signed on voyages to Guinea, Madeira and Porto Santo, observing the methods of Portuguese captains and navigators and studying their instruments and sea charts until he became a skilled navigator.

Presently he came to the conclusion that the best and shortest way to reach the rich rewards of India and the Spice Islands was not by rounding Africa and sailing east, but by setting a westward course from Europe. Nobody suspected that two huge continents, North and South America, lay between Europe and China and India; the geographers believed that the Orient lay just across the Atlantic Ocean.

In 1480 Columbus approached King John of Portugal with his new idea, and a request that he supply Columbus with ships and men to make such a voyage for Portugal, but he was refused. Some say he demanded too much reward; he wanted to be knighted, made viceroy of any new lands, named Admiral of the Oceans and to receive one tenth of all revenues. Others thought the King refused because his courtiers persuaded him to send his own ships to carry out Columbus' plans and freeze him out of the whole venture. At any rate Columbus left Lisbon in anger and went to Spain. King Ferdinand and Queen Isabella financed that memorable first voyage of discovery to America and the West Indies, which he thought were the islands of Japan.

When Columbus returned triumphantly and put in at Lisbon on the way to Spain, King John felt that the newly discovered islands should belong to Portugal, because in a treaty with Spain in 1481, the King of Spain had agreed not to claim any territory south of Cape Bojador except the Canaries. When Ferdinand learned of John's claim he petitioned the Pope in Rome to settle the dispute, which after some haggling resulted in the treaty of Tordesillas, June 4th 1494. This treaty stated that all new territories east of a line running along the 46th meridian of West Longitude and west of a line along the 134th meridian, East Longitude, should belong to Portugal, while everything on the opposite sides of those lines would belong to Spain. The map of the Portuguese explorations of the sixteenth century show clearly how the Pope carved up the world between Spain and Portugal by these Treaty lines, although he had not the slightest right to any of the territory. Of course this highhanded decision lasted only as long as no other country disputed it. Soon England, France and Holland would be sending out their galleons to raid Spanish and Portuguese shipping and many of their colonial towns and ports. But, during the fifteenth and sixteenth centuries the Portuguese and Spaniards were masters of the seas.

In 1495 a new King, Manuel I, ascended the throne of Portugal. He was eager to complete the task of finding the sea route to India started by Prince Henry. By this time Bartolomeo Diaz had built several ships of the new type he believed suitable for such long voyages. The *São Gabriel,* of 120 tons, was either a carrack or perhaps one of the new galleons, as was the *São Rafael,* of 100 tons, while the *Berrio* was a four masted caravel with a square-rigged foremast, of 50 tons. There was also a barco to carry supplies.

In 1495, just before his death, King John had selected Estevão da Gama to be commander of the new expedition, but Estevão died before the fleet was ready to sail. The King then named his son, Vasco da Gama, a man in his thirties, as commander of the expedition and captain of the *São Gabriel* with the famous Pero de Alenquer as his chief pilot. The *São Rafael* was commanded by Vasco's brother Paulo, the captain of the *Berrio* was Nicolau Coelho, and Gonçalo Nunes commanded the store ship.

The little fleet assembled in the Tagus just below Lisbon, where, amid a great crowd of well-wishers, the King bade goodbye to da Gama and his officers. On July 8th 1497, the ships weighed anchor and trimmed their yards to catch the northeast breeze. Opposite Cape Verde, the ships laid a course far west of the African coast to avoid unfavorable winds and currents, which took them on an incredible cruise of 4500 miles during which they were out of sight of land for ninety-six days. This was by far the longest sea voyage in history, far longer than Columbus', from Spain to the West Indies.

Their first landfall was a place they named St. Helena Bay on the southwest coast of Africa, which they reached on November 8th, for a two days' stay. They rounded the Cape of Good Hope and presently passed the last pillar, left by Diaz. By now many of the men were down with scurvy caused by lack of fresh food, the water in their casks was becoming too foul to drink, and the salt meat and biscuits were running low. They had to find new supplies quickly.

Remembering Covilha's letter to King John, in which he told of visiting Sofala and other east coast Moslem ports, da Gama sailed northward, missing Sofala, but presently came to Mozambique, a bustling Arab town, where they obtained provisions, and fresh fruit and vegetables to cure the scurvy. They spent a month there cleaning the ships' bottoms and repairing rigging. At Mozambique they saw many Arab ships coming and going, laden with cargoes of gold and silver, rubies and pearls, pepper, ginger, cloves and other rare spices. For a while they were well treated at Mozambique, but when the sheik who ruled the port learned they were Christians they had to leave in a hurry.

They put into the next Arab port up the coast, Mombasa, but here the whole expedition was almost destroyed by Mohammedans who hated all Christians. They managed to escape and headed for Malindi, a short distance up the coast, where they found the Sultan to be friendly, although he too was a Mohammedan. When they dropped anchor he sent out a gift of three sheep, and invited them to enter the port. Not to be outdone, da Gama sent the King a cassock, three wash basins, a crimson hat, several strings of coral and some bells.

Presently the Sultan, in a green satin-trimmed damask robe and a jeweled turban, and sheltered under a crimson satin umbrella, was rowed out to the *São Gabriel* for a formal visit. The Sultan was eager to establish trade with the Portuguese, and entertained them lavishly in Malindi, whose tall, whitewashed houses standing in beautiful gardens along the bay, reminded the men of their own home towns.

After a pleasant stay of nine days, da Gama ordered the anchors catted and the little fleet set out on the last

leg of their history-making voyage, with fabulous India as their goal. Guided by an Indian from Gujerat, supplied by the Sultan, they sailed for twenty-three days across the Arabian Gulf without sighting land.

On the twenty-fourth day, a dim blue line of rugged mountains appeared on the horizon; their long-sought goal, India, lay before them. On May 21st, 1498, almost eleven months after they left the harbor of Lisbon, the little ships dropped their anchors at Calicut.

Vasco da Gama sent several of his officers ashore with their interpreter to bring greetings from King Manuel to the Samuri, ruler of Calicut, and beg leave to be allowed to come ashore. Permission was granted and on the 28th of May, 1498, Vasco and thirteen of his men landed and made their way along the crowded streets lined with wooden houses thatched with palm

leaves to the Samuri's palace. They were led into his audience chamber where he awaited them under a gilded canopy, lying on a couch covered with a richly embroidered green velvet cloth. Vasco told the Samuri of his country and of his great King, lord of many lands and wealthier than any king of India. He laid before the Samuri presents of coral, sugar, oil, scarlet cloth and red hats, but the presents were treated with amused contempt, as being too paltry to offer a great monarch. However the Samuri remained friendly and gave permission for the Portuguese to trade with the Calicut merchants.

Still, all went far from well with the Portuguese. Calicut was full of Arab merchants who had always

enjoyed a monopoly in the trading of spices, rugs, silks and jewels with Europe. Their caravans and ships carried these products of the East to the Mediterranean where the merchants of the Italian maritime cities, Genoa and Venice, bought them to distribute throughout Europe. Neither the Arabs or the Italian merchants were eager to see the Portuguese bring back this profitable merchandise directly to Europe by sea.

The Arabs began bringing false tales of the secret plans of the Portuguese to overthrow the Samuri, which caused him to withdraw his friendship. The Portuguese thereupon began to be attacked by Arab bullies in the streets, and finally da Gama and some of his men were arrested and imprisoned. He managed to escape and sailed down the coast to trade with more peaceful Indian ports.

At last he left India with a small cargo of spices and other valuable merchandise and began the long voyage home. On the way fever and scurvy broke out among the crews and soon there were not enough men to work all the ships. The little provision barco had already been unloaded and broken up; now off Mozambique, the *São Rafael* had to be abandoned and burned for lack of crew to work her. Only the *São Gabriel* and *Berrio* remained to round the Cape of Good Hope on March 20th, 1499.

The *Berrio* reached Lisbon first, in July. Da Gama headed for the Azores, hoping in vain that the fine climate there might save his brother, who was dying aboard the *São Gabriel*. Vasco arrived in the Tagus in

76

September, to be greeted by the King, who had heard the wonderful news of the voyage, and saw, as proof, the rubies, pearls and gold, the cloves, ginger, nutmeg and other cargo the ships had brought back. Vasco was made Admiral of India and Count of Vidiguerra, and given a pension of 3000 ducats a year; later he was made Viceroy of India.

After hearing da Gama's report of his voyage, the King decided to lose no time in building up Portugal's fortunes by trading with the Far East. Strangely enough, instead of offering the command of the next fleet to da Gama, he gave it to one Pedro Alvares Cabral. In March, 1500 Cabral left Lisbon in command of a fleet of thirteen well-armed vessels manned by over fifteen hundred men. As second in command he had the veteran Bartolomeo Diaz, and among his crew were eight Franciscan friars to convert the unbelievers, eight chaplains, a number of skilled gunners to work the ships' bombards, and a group of merchants with trade goods to barter in Calicut.

King Manuel who now was titled "King by the Grace of God of Portugal, and of Algarves, both on the side of the Sea and Beyond it to Africa, Lord of Guinea and of the Conquest, Navigation and Commerce of Ethiopia, Arabia, Persia and India" came down to the harbor to see Cabral off, and present him with a banner emblazoned with the Royal Arms of Portugal. For some reason Cabral's fleet took a more southwesterly course after leaving the Cape Verdes than had any of the previous explorers, and presently on April 22, 1500, the

lookouts sighted new land. Upon going ashore the sailors described it as a fruitful country, full of trees, and

inhabited by swarthy people who were armed with bows and arrows. They exchanged some sheets of paper and bolts of cloth for tame parrots and called their find "The Land of the Holy Cross." Later they learned that it had already been discovered several years before by Pinzon, one of Columbus' captains, who had named it Brazil. The coast of Brazil lay to the east of the Treaty line, and so belonged to Portugal; Cabral sent one ship back to Lisbon to report its discovery, while the rest of the fleet sailed on toward the Cape of Good Hope.

Soon after they rounded the Cape and headed toward the Indian Ocean a violent storm overwhelmed them: when the weather abated it was found that four of the ships had foundered with all hands, among them Bartolomeo Diaz, who was fated to perish without ever seeing India.

After making emergency repairs and reassembling, the fleet bore on, discovering the great island of Madagascar on the way, and finally in September dropped anchor at Calicut. Cabral was reluctantly received by the Samuri, who by now had been won over by the Arab traders and was cool toward the Portuguese. The Samuri wore a glittering costume and jewelry to impress Cabral. He wore a cap of gold and a pair of earrings composed of diamonds, sapphires and pearls, two of which were larger than walnuts. His arms and legs were loaded with bracelets set with valuable jewels and his fingers and toes were covered with rings set with huge diamonds and rubies. Most dazzling of all

was his girdle, covered with precious stones set in gold.

The Samuri grudgingly turned over a house at the waterside to Cabral to be used as a depot for trading with the local merchants and to store the spices he would buy. For a short time all went well, then a riot broke out and the furious Arabs attacked the depot and killed all the Portuguese in it. In revenge Cabral's fleet bombarded the city and set it afire before they left to trade with the friendlier natives at Cochin and Cananor on the Malabar coast. After trading along the coast for some time and filling their holds they set sail for Lisbon, but so great were the hardships of the voyage that Cabral's fleet was reduced from thirteen ships to six by the time they anchored in the Tagus.

Before Cabral's return the King had sent out a fleet of four ships on a trading mission; their most important contribution was the discovery of Ascension and St. Helena, two tiny islands in the middle of the South Atlantic. They were important to King Manuel because they became two more of the chain of safe ports, like Madeira and the Cape Verdes, where his little treasure ships could put in for food, water and repairs between Lisbon and India.

Every year now a new fleet was dispatched to India, often to meet with disaster from storms and battles with the natives, but many ships returned with holds filled with spices and other valuable cargo to enrich Portugal. The captains were constantly learning better routes for their ships; learning when to leave Lisbon to arrive in East Africa just as the seasonal monsoons started blowing from the southwest to carry them across the Indian Ocean to Hindustan, and when to leave India for the northeast monsoon to blow them back around the Cape.

They soon found that India was not the source of the rarer spices, such as nutmeg and cloves. Ginger was produced in Malabar but it was not very valuable, while cinnamon came from Ceylon and the really rare cloves and nutmeg grew in the mysterious Spice Islands, somewhere still further to the east. The Portuguese saw that if they expected to corner the spice trade they would have to capture Aden at the foot of the Red Sea, Ormuz on the Persian Gulf, and the Malaccan Straits, to keep the Arabs from shipping spices to the Mediterranean. A look at a map of the Portuguese explorations shows how easily the Portuguese could have blocked the Arabs if they held those places. As it turned out, they were never able to capture Aden, so the Red Sea route could always be used by the Arabs. Even then the Portuguese almost succeeded; in 1504 when Venetian and Genoese galleys arrived in Beirut and Alexandria to buy spices, they found that the Arab caravaneers had none to sell; the Portuguese had bought all the spices in India.

By 1505 the Portuguese ships knew the Arabian Sea and the coasts of India, Persia and Arabia as well as the East African coast. They put in to all the harbors and traded with the natives, establishing small forts where their merchants could store goods and defend themselves if they were attacked. Now King Manuel decided it was time to subdue the native kings and take possession of their lands.

The Portuguese Empire began when Manuel named Francisco de Almeida his Viceroy in India and sent him there with instructions to build strong forts all along the African and Indian coasts. Meanwhile the constant demand for sailors to man the ships was beginning to exhaust the supply. Portugal was a very small country with a population of less than two million. Almeida had to be satisfied with green countrymen who had never been aboard a ship and were so ignorant they hardly knew right from left, much less starboard from larboard. To train the raw landsmen to steer, he had a bunch of onions tied to the starboard rail and a bunch of garlic to the larboard; the pilot would then shout to the helmsman, "Onion your helm" or "Garlic your helm."

One by one the native cities fell to the Portuguese, who were better fighters and sailors than the Hindus or Arabs. Almeida made Cochin his headquarters, from which his son Lorenzo sailed forth and discovered the island of Ceylon, off the tip of India, where he set up a marble pillar to mark the easternmost point of the Portuguese Empire. From here Lorenzo sent back to Lisbon the first elephant ever seen in Portugal. Shortly afterward the brilliant young commander was killed in action.

Almeida still had to face a threat from a combined Arab and Indian fleet to the north at Diu. In 1509 he fought the longest battle in the history of Portu-

guese India and utterly routed the enemy. Afonso de
Albuquerque was now named Viceroy to take over
from Almeida; he was a strong and forceful man, des-
tined to establish the great Portuguese Indian Empire

firmly. As soon as he arrived, in reprisal for continual attacks on the Portuguese by the Samuri of Calicut, he bombarded and burned his city to the ground in 1510.

Albuquerque decided that the city of Goa would be the best place for his capital, so he attacked it, and after desperate fighting during which it changed hands three times, captured Goa. It remained in Portuguese hands for four hundred and fifty years. His next step was to close off the trade routes from the East to any but Portuguese controlled ships. He sent an expedition to besiege Malacca, which guarded the straits between Sumatra and Malaya and conquered it after heavy fighting.

Strange tales came back from Sumatra; sailors told of cannibals who found the flesh of black men sweeter than that of white men, of finding people with tails like sheep, of hens with pitch black flesh, and of rivers of oil.

85

The fall of Malacca was a red-letter day for the Portuguese; now the route to those fabulous Spice Islands where the rare cloves and nutmegs grew was open at last. Malacca was also the gateway for all the rich products of the Philippines, Japan and China, silks and embroideries, tea, porcelain, exquisite carvings, sandalwood and many other Oriental goods. The Sultan of conquered Malacca escaped and sent a vain plea to the Ming Emperor of China to take action against these white aggressors who were overrunning the East Indies. Wu Tang, the Son of Heaven, did nothing but issue a decree scolding the white men and ordering the King of Siam, one of his vassals, to drive them away. However the ruler of Siam had quarreled with the Sultan of Malacca, and refused to attack the Portuguese; instead they exchanged missions, gave each other gifts and stayed on friendly terms.

King Manuel wrote the Pope about his new conquest, and on November 3rd, 1514, the Pope issued a bull forbidding any other Christian nation to trespass or interfere with Manuel's new territories. Albuquerque's next move was to send envoys to Java and order a small fleet to search for the Moluccas, the famous Spice Islands.

Francisco Serrano, a Portuguese captain, was the first white man to see them, in 1511. He told of passing island after island, all rich in spices and wrote to his friend Ferdinand Magellan, who was soon to sail around the world, that he had found yet another new world larger and richer than that found by da Gama. Presently strange stories reached Lisbon about those Moluccas, of rivers of boiling water in which were living fish, of hogs with horns, of hens that laid their eggs nine feet underground, and of poisonous crabs and oysters with mammoth shells. The men of these islands were reputed to have spurs growing from their ankles.

Soon these intrepid explorers were reaching still farther. After the death of Albuquerque, Tomé Pires set out for China and appeared at Canton, where he

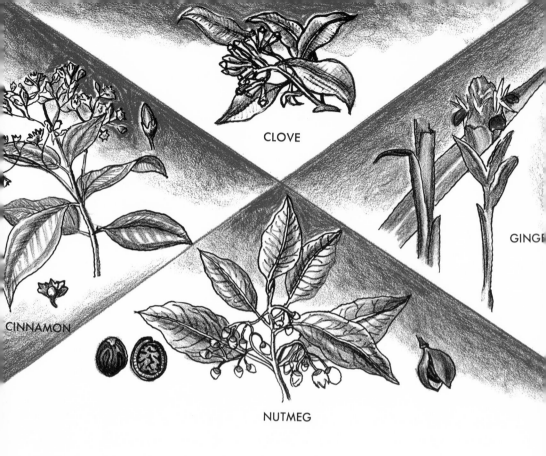

CLOVE

GING[

CINNAMON

NUTMEG

was coldly received by the Chinese who thought all foreigners were not good enough to tread on Chinese soil. Pires did manage to get permission to establish a foothold at Macao on the Chinese mainland at the mouth of the river where Canton lay, and Macao has remained an important trading post for the Portuguese to this day. It is recorded that three Portuguese sailors even visited Japan before 1550.

Portuguese sea-rovers were busy on the other side of the world also, making exploratory voyages westward in the North Atlantic. Gaspar Corte-Real, born in the

Azores, and so a Portuguese citizen, discovered the island of Newfoundland in 1500 and called it Tierra de los Bacalaos, or the Land of the Codfish. A year later while on a second voyage his ship was wrecked and he was lost at sea, but not before his report on the fishing banks had reached the ears of Portuguese fishing captains. From that time to the present day Portuguese fishing fleets have crossed the stormy Atlantic every year to hand-line for cod off the bleak shores of Newfoundland and later, Greenland.

In 1521 King Manuel, who had reigned for twenty-six years, died. During those years Portugal, a small state with only a few island colonies, had grown into a great world empire, with possessions stretching around Africa to India and beyond to the East Indies. Portuguese ships ranged over thousands of miles of sea routes, bringing rich cargoes from half the world to Lisbon. Manuel's palaces and his court were the most splendid in Europe, and the great voyages of da Gama, Almeida and Albuquerque were known and respected by all Europe. It seemed that Portugal would remain strong and prosperous forever.

Yet when the new King, João III ascended the throne in 1521, at the age of twenty for a reign of almost thirty-six years, his ministers found the treasury almost empty. They discovered that the vast Empire cost more to run than it brought in. Fitting out a ship for a voyage to India was expensive, and at best such a vessel was good for only a few round 'trips before it wore out. Many ships were wrecked or lost at sea during early voyages, so they and their cargoes were a total loss. The warships which guarded the Empire brought no profits to the Crown. They were a heavy expense, as were the troops and forts dotted along the coasts, and the host of high-salaried governors and officials. From Vasco da Gama's time until the end of Manuel's reign only about a dozen ships a year made the voyage to India and some of these were lost; they were not enough to carry all the spices and other eastern merchandise Europe needed. Also many of Portugal's best young men were drained off every year to serve in the colonies, some to die or return in broken health, others to go native. Fortunes were made, but not by the soldiers, sailors and officials, but rather by foreign bankers and middlemen who took mortgages on the goods and resold them. In a word, the Portuguese Colonial Empire was run for the enrichment of others.

To make matters worse, French, British and Dutch privateers were ranging the seas, attacking and looting Portuguese and Spanish ships wherever they found them, and raiding their ports in the East; these raiders were not bound by the Pope's treaties. French corsairs began to use the harbors along the Brazilian coast as bases from which to dart out and attack the undermanned homeward bound spice ships which could not escape because their sails and rigging were damaged and their bottoms fouled with weeds and barnacles after the long voyage.

Although the Portuguese had never colonized their

Brazilian territory João realized he would have to establish a permanent settlement there, if only to drive away the raiders. In 1530 he sent a small fleet under Martim Afonso da Sousa to survey the coast and begin a permanent settlement at a good place, and also drive out any intruders he found. He did discover some Frenchmen whom he drove out, and also Castilian and Portuguese pioneers who had made their homes along the coast. For some reason he missed the fine harbor at what is now Rio de Janiero, and located his first settlement at São Vicente, near present day Santos, in 1532. Soon afterwards he returned to Lisbon, and was presently appointed Viceroy of India.

The King soon found that one settlement on a coastline thousands of miles long was no protection against the corsairs, but his treasury was too poor to permit the government to do anything further. He therefore divided up the coast into fifteen grants, or capitanias, and awarded them to nobles or wealthy men, each of whom was to be responsible for bringing colonists to his own capitania, and supplying their needs while they were getting started. Some of these grantees or donataries managed to start flourishing settlements but others failed, often because of hostile Indians and poor management.

It was soon seen that these capitanias needed one strong head, so in 1549 the King appointed Tomé da Sousa governor-general to rule all Brazil. He made Baia (Bahia) his capital and brought in officials, soldiers, more colonists and Jesuit friars to convert the

Indians. He arrived just in time, because the French had already started a settlement at Rio de Janeiro, hoping to establish a great colonial empire of their own which they called "Antarctica France." Because of quarrels among themselves the French outpost was weakened and finally da Sousa was able to destroy it. Except for a strong Dutch colony which was finally defeated the Portuguese held Brazil until the colonists themselves revolted and became independent.

Meanwhile in Portugal a new King, Sebastião, reigned. He was ambitious and eager to head a new crusade against the Moors in Morocco. Against the advice of his council he raised an army of over twenty thousand men, and in 1578 landed his troops in Morocco. The Moors retreated until the Portuguese army was deep in the dry, hot hills, exhausted and thirsty. Then they struck and annihilated Sebastião's troops. The young King was killed and most of his army was captured and had to be ransomed at a high cost. The nation was so weakened that Philip II of Spain was able to invade Portugal and force it to accept him as its King in 1581. Portugal remained under Spanish rule for sixty years, and during this time her Indian Empire declined steadily. The Dutch sent their own ships to India and took away most of the Portuguese trade. Then they established their own forts in the East, raiding Portuguese ships and harbors constantly. Eventually they captured most of the East Indies, and the Dutch East Indies Company supplanted the Portuguese Empire. All that remained was the tiny colony of Macao, which remains so to this day. The Moroccans and later the Spanish and French wrested her north African possessions, including Ceuta and Tangier, from Portugal, leaving her only the Azores, Madeira, the Cape Verdes and Goa, former capital of her Empire. Goa was bloodlessly annexed by the newly independent India in the mid-twentieth century. Brazil overthrew its Emperor Pedro, a member of the Portuguese Royal Family, in 1889 and became a republic, which broke the last tie between the Mother country and her Brazilian possessions.

By the nineteenth century Portugal's vast Empire was reduced to Angola on the west Coast and Mozambique on the east. In Africa these are among the last of the colonies seized by European nations in the nineteenth century which have not yet been given their independence. When they win their freedom, which seems only a matter of time, the last vestiges of the greatest colonial empire of the fifteenth and sixteenth centuries built by the Portuguese explorers, will have vanished forever.

Contents

John III, King of Portugal, 89, 91

log, ship's, 28

Macao, 88, 93
Madeira, 39, 40 ff., 68, 81, 93
Magellan, Ferdinand, 87
Malacca, 85-86, 87
Malindi, 72-74
Manuel I, King of Portugal, 70, 74, 77, 81, 82-83, 89, 90
Mohammedans, 6, 72
Moluccas (Spice Islands), 10 ff., 69, 86, 87
Moors, 12, 16 ff., 43-44, 48-49, 92
Mozambique, 13, 71-72

navigation, celestial, 28 ff.
Newfoundland, 7, 88-89

Paiva, 65, 66
Pedro, King of Portugal, 15-16, 18, 20, 49
Perestrello, 39
Phoenicians, 13, 32
Pires, Tomé, 87-88
Porto Santo, 38 ff., 68
Prester John, 64, 66

Red Sea route, 12, 82
Rio de Ouro, 48, 50, 52

St. Helena Island, 81
Sala-ben-Sala, 22, 24
Santa Maria, 44-45
Sebastian, King of Portugal, 92
Serrano, Francisco, 87
ships, 32 ff., 68, 70, 89-90
slave trade, 53, 61
Sofala, 66, 71
Spanish, 8, 69-70, 92, 93
Spice Islands, 10 ff., 69, 86, 87
spice trade, 10 ff., 61, 72, 74-75, 81, 82, 90
Sumatra, 85

Teixiera, Tristão Vaz, 38 ff.
Timbuktoo, 12, 52
Tordesillas, Treaty of, 69
trade routes, 11 ff., 52-53, 58-59, 61 ff., 68-69, 81 ff., 84, 86
Tristão, Nuno, 50-51, 55, 60

West Indies, 69, 71

Zarco, João Gonçalves, 38 ff.

The Author and Artist

WALTER BUEHR is a favorite author-illustrator of many young people. His books on the romantic periods of history deal with the crusades, knighthood, galleys and galleons. He is also the author of a series of books on early explorers in America and now adds the Portuguese explorers to his list.

Mr. Buehr and his wife, Camilla, who is a fashion illustrator, divide their time between Abaco in the West Indies and Noroton, Connecticut.